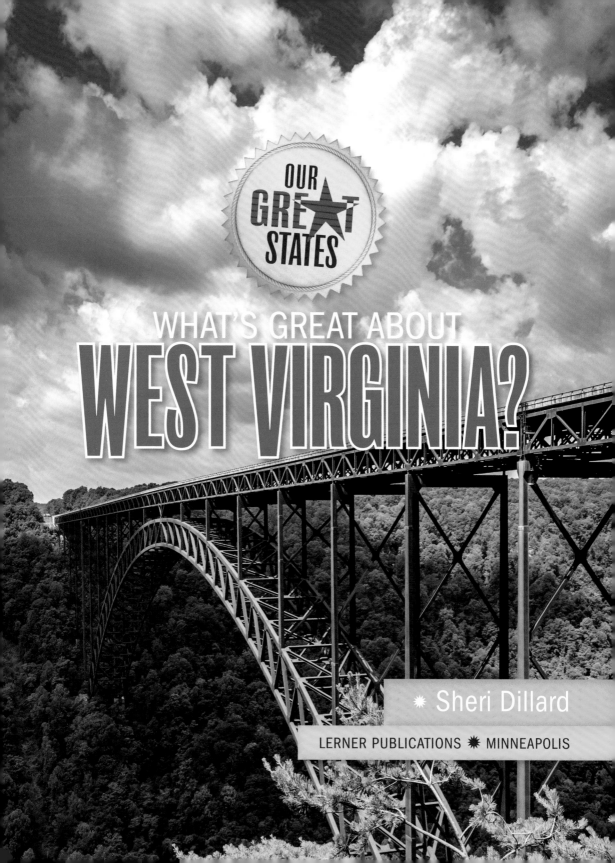

OUR
GR★AT
STATES

WHAT'S GREAT ABOUT
WEST VIRGINIA?

✳ Sheri Dillard

LERNER PUBLICATIONS ✳ MINNEAPOLIS

CONTENTS

Copyright © 2016
by Lerner Publishing Group, Inc.

Content Consultant: Dr. Billy Joe Peyton
Professor of History, West Virginia State
University

Lerner Publications Company
A division of Lerner Publishing Group, Inc.
241 First Avenue North
Minneapolis, MN 55401 USA

For reading levels and more information, look
up this title at www.lernerbooks.com.

Main body text set in ITC Franklin Gothic Std
Book Condensed 12/15.
Typeface provided by Adobe Systems.

**Library of Congress Cataloging-in-Publication
Data**

The Cataloging-in-Publication Data for *What's
Great about West Virginia?* is on file at the
Library of Congress.

ISBN 978-1-4677-3877-4 (lib. bdg.)
ISBN 978-1-4677-8519-8 (pbk.)
ISBN 978-1-4677-8520-4 (EB pdf)

Manufactured in the United States of America
1 – PC – 7/15/15

WEST VIRGINIA Welcomes You!

Welcome to the Mountain State! All of West Virginia is in the Appalachian Mountain range. And there is plenty of outdoor fun here! Explore gorges as you speed through whitewater rapids. On a sunny summer day, hike or bike the state's many trails. You can even zip-line through forests. Come in the winter and ski or sled your way down a mountainside. Or ride a train around and over a mountain. You might even venture below the mountains to check out caverns and a coal mine. There are many fun ways to experience West Virginia. Read on to find out about ten things that make this state great!

Explore West Virginia's mountains and all the places in between! Just turn the page to find out about THE MOUNTAIN STATE. >

PENNSYLVANIA

MARYLAND

OHIO

Weirton

Weirton Heights

Wheeling

Ohio River

Morgantown

Fairmont

Parkersburg

Martinsburg

A L L E G H E N Y   M O U N T A I N S

Spruce Knob
(4,861 feet/
1,482 m)

Charleston

New River

Huntington

Kanawha River

VIRGINIA

Beckley

Greenbrier River

KENTUCKY

Guyandotte River

Miles
0   20   40   60

0   20   40   60   80
Kilometers

BLACKWATER FALLS STATE PARK

> Make your first stop Blackwater Falls State Park in Davis. This amazing state park has something for everyone. Do you like exploring woods? Hike the more than 20 miles (32 kilometers) of trails. Other fun options include fishing, camping, and boating. Then check out Blackwater Falls. This impressive waterfall is 60 feet (18 meters) tall. It is also one of the most photographed places in the state. Walk out on a platform to snap the perfect shot without getting wet.

If you come in the winter, Blackwater Falls is just as much fun in the snow. Travel the hiking trails on cross-country skis. Then grab a sled. The Blackwater Falls Sled Run has been open since 1960. Snowmaking equipment makes every day a sledding day. Hop on the Wonder Carpet conveyor and be whisked to the top of the hill with your sled. Once you reach the top, zoom down the 0.25-mile (0.4 km) sledding trail. Then jump back on the conveyor and do it all again! Do you need a break from sledding? Enjoy hot drinks and homemade soups and stews at the warming hut.

Catch a view of Blackwater Canyon from Lindy Point in Blackwater Falls State Park.

Camp and roast marshmallows at Blackwater Falls.

CASS SCENIC RAILROAD STATE PARK

> All aboard! Hop on a real steam train at Cass Scenic Railroad State Park in Cass. The steam whistle shrieks as you start to move. Watch clouds of black smoke float by as you pick up speed on your way up the mountain. Bring your friends and family. You can reserve an entire train car for your group. Each car can seat about thirty-five people. Remember to bring a jacket because the mountain air blowing into the cars is cool!

The Cass Scenic Railroad travels on the same line that brought wood to sawmills more than one hundred years ago. The train's first stop is Whittaker Station. It is an area built to look like a logging camp from the 1940s. Don't miss the Lidgerwood tower skidder. This huge machine carried giant logs out of the woods. The second stop is Bald Knob, one of the highest points in West Virginia. Cass Scenic Railroad State Park also rents out equipment for tubing, fishing, and biking along the nearby Greenbrier River Trail.

You'll have an amazing view of the state's landscape from Bald Knob.

RAILROAD HISTORY

Have you ever played the board game Monopoly? The B&O Railroad space is named after the Baltimore & Ohio Railroad. It's the oldest railroad in the United States. In 1852, the B&O Railroad line was finished. Much of the route was in West Virginia. Railroads created paths to the mountains. This made it easier to get important natural resources such as lumber and coal out of the mountain areas.

HATFIELD-McCOY TRAILS

> West Virginia has many trails for walking, biking, and horseback riding. But the Hatfield-McCoy Trail System has a different type of trail in nine southern West Virginia counties. These trails are perfect for dirt bikes, all-terrain vehicles (ATVs), and utility task vehicles (UTVs). All of these vehicles are driven off-road. And they are lots of fun! Rev up and ride on more than 700 miles (1,127 km) of off-road trails. Many of the towns in the area are ATV-friendly too.

You can rent a vehicle or bring your own. There are also guided tours of the trails. The Ivy Branch trail allows bigger vehicles, such as Jeeps and trucks. If you are at least eight years old, you can ride as a passenger. Buckle up! It's sure to be a wild ride!

Enjoy the Hatfield-McCoy
trails on an ATV.

THE HATFIELDS AND THE McCOYS

In the 1800s, the Hatfield family lived in southwestern West Virginia. The McCoy family lived in eastern Kentucky. The two large families were involved in a feud. People tell different stories about how the feud started. One theory is that the families were on opposite sides during the Civil War (1861–1865). Another tale includes a stolen pig. But however the feud started, it became very violent. Several family members were killed in fights. Others ended up in jail. People in West Virginia still tell stories of the families' historic feud.

NEW RIVER GORGE NATIONAL RIVER

> The New River is actually very old! Many scientists think it's one of the oldest rivers on Earth. The New River Gorge National River is a 53-mile (85 km) section of the river. Whitewater rafting is popular here. Visit Adventures on the Gorge for rafting. Hop in a raft for a gentle trip down the river. If you are a thrill-seeker, try the part of the river that cuts through the heart of the gorge. Huge waves and big drops take you on a wild ride through this quick-flowing section. Pass under the majestic New River Gorge Bridge.

This fascinating bridge is one of the world's longest steel span bridges. On the third Saturday in October, the people of West Virginia celebrate Bridge Day. This is the only day of the year that you can walk across the top of the bridge. Will you make the 3,030-foot (924 m) trip? Look down into the gorge. The river is 876 feet (267 m) below! More than eighty thousand people celebrate Bridge Day, which includes food, music, and a festival. Every day of the year, a catwalk below the bridge is open for walking tours.

Watch people parachute off the New River Gorge Bridge on Bridge Day!

Travel down the New River in a one- or two-person raft called a ducky.

EXHIBITION COAL MINE

> The Exhibition Coal Mine in Beckley is your chance to go below West Virginia's mountains! The Phillips-Sprague mine was a working coal mine from 1889 to 1953. It opened as an exhibition mine in 1962. Board a mantrip for your ride through the mine. A mantrip is a shuttle used to take miners into the mines. Be sure to stay in your seat! The mine roof is just above your head. The tour guides are real coal miners themselves. They'll tell you about the dangers of coal mining and explain how coal miners blasted holes in the mountain to bring out the coal. The temperature in the dark mine is always a chilly 58°F (14°C). Bring a jacket!

Before you leave, stop by the Exhibition Mine's coal camp. Here you'll see what life was like for miners in the early 1900s. The miners lived in the coal camp with their families. The coal company owned the buildings, including homes, a store, a church, and a school. You can tour the restored school, church, and homes.

WHAT IS COAL?

Coal is made up of plants that lived millions of years ago. As the plants died, they started to break down. Over time, layers of dirt, mud, rock, and water buried the dead plants. Pressure and heat caused the layers to physically change, turning the layers of material into coal. Coal is used for many things. It can be burned to make heat and electricity. It is also used to make steel and energy.

See the old church at the Exhibition Coal Mine's coal camp.

CLAY CENTER FOR THE ARTS AND SCIENCES

> Make the Clay Center for the Arts and Sciences of West Virginia in Charleston your next stop. Before going into the Clay Center, walk through the Sculpture Garden. Artists from around the world show their work here. Inside the center, more than 9,000 square feet (836 sq. m) of galleries fill the building. The art gallery has works by well-known artists such as Andy Warhol and Pablo Picasso.

If you're a science lover, check out the center's Avampato Discovery Museum. Live science shows are held each day. The museum is filled with hands-on science exhibits too. At Milton Gardner's Earth City, explore the forces behind tornados and geysers. And don't miss the ElectricSky Theater with its domed screen! Sit back in your seat. Then look up. The giant screen will make you think you're in a real volcano or ocean. Finish your visit with a journey through the galaxy at one of the center's planetarium shows.

An artist poses with his model of Dr. Seuss's *The Lorax*.

Watch your step as you cross a bridge of logs at TimberTrek Aerial Adventure Park.

TIMBERTREK AERIAL ADVENTURE PARK

> Adventures on the Gorge's TimberTrek Aerial Adventure Park in Lansing offers an exciting way to explore West Virginia. It's a playground in the treetops! You'll cross bridges and speed down zip lines. Swings and platforms help you work your way through the trees. The highest platform is 50 feet (15 m) above the ground. Crawl through wooden tunnels and walk across a chain bridge. It's a self-guided course. Go as slowly or as quickly as you want!

Take to the trees at night! Challenge yourself to the same course at night on a MoonTrek. Stringed lights line the bridges as you crawl through the course.

Gloves, helmets, and harnesses keep you safe as you explore the treetops.

GOOD ZOO & BENEDUM THEATER

> Good Zoo & Benedum Theater in Wheeling really is a good zoo! See bears, meerkats, red pandas, and other fun animals. At the Discovery Lab, you'll see smaller animals, such as salamanders and poison dart frogs. In the Benedum Theater, watch videos about nature.

Then head outside. You can explore the zoo by train. A 1.5-mile (2.4 km) track loops around the park. In the Wonders of the Wetlands section, you'll see cranes and bald eagles. You'll find friendly goats, pigs, and donkeys in the red barn. Be sure to sign up for an Animal Encounter. This program lets you join a zookeeper during feeding time. Help the worker feed and train the animals. You can choose to help out with lemurs or river otters. Finish off your day by visiting lorikeets at Lorikeet Landing.

The red panda is just one of the animals you'll meet at Good Zoo.

Give a lemur a snack as part of Good Zoo's Animal Encounter program.

GHOST TOUR OF HARPERS FERRY

Your guide will walk you through historic Harpers Ferry, sharing spooky tales.

> Harpers Ferry is a town with a lot of history and many ghost stories. The Ghost Tour of Harpers Ferry is one of the oldest ghost tours in the United States. People have been taking this tour for more than forty years! Bring your flashlight. Prepare to be spooked as you explore the town of Harpers Ferry at night.

The tour is based on Shirley Dougherty's 1977 book *A Ghostly Tour of Harpers Ferry*. Dougherty was spooked by scary events that happened in the restaurant she owned. She wanted an explanation. As she researched, she learned that many townspeople had their own spooky stories—enough to fill a book! One spooky story involves Harpers Ferry's St. Peters Catholic Church, which towers high above the town. During the Civil War, this church served as a hospital. It is said that one soldier who died in the hospital still visits and can be heard speaking.

JOHN BROWN

In 1859, a man named John Brown led a raid in Harpers Ferry. Brown was a white abolitionist. He wanted to put an end to slavery in the United States. He gathered twenty-one men who felt the same way. Then, on October 16, 1859, he and his men attacked a building that was filled with weapons. His goal was to give weapons to slaves so that they could fight against slavery. His plan didn't work. Many of his men were killed. But Brown's actions led others to think about whether slavery was right or wrong.

SNOWSHOE MOUNTAIN

Snowshoe Mountain's slopes are perfect for snowboarding.

> If you visit West Virginia in winter, bundle up! Then head to Snowshoe Mountain in Pocahontas County. This ski resort has more than 250 acres (100 hectares) of snowy winter fun! Check out some of the resort's fifty-seven skiing and snowboarding trails. Easier runs are available for beginning skiers.

After skiing, use a snowmobile to explore other areas. Or head to the Coca-Cola Tube Park. This tubing hill is six stories high! For something a little different, take a tour of the trails on a snowcat. The slopes can get choppy and messy over time. On this tour, you'll see how workers use snowcat trucks to keep the snow perfect for skiing. The workers can even make snow if they have to! You'll visit the Snowshoe Compressor House. See the equipment they use to turn the water from Shaver's Lake into snow.

Are you just learning to ski? Try Snowshoe Mountain's beginner trails.

YOUR TOP TEN

Now that you've read about ten awesome things to see and do in West Virginia, think about what your West Virginia top ten list would include. What would you like to see if you visited the state? What would you like to do there? If you'd like, you can even turn your list into a book and illustrate it with drawings or with pictures from the Internet or magazines.

WEST VIRGINIA BY MAP

Huntington

Hatfield-McCoy Trails

Visit www.lerneresource.com to learn more about the state flag of West Virginia.

STATE OF WEST VIRGINIA

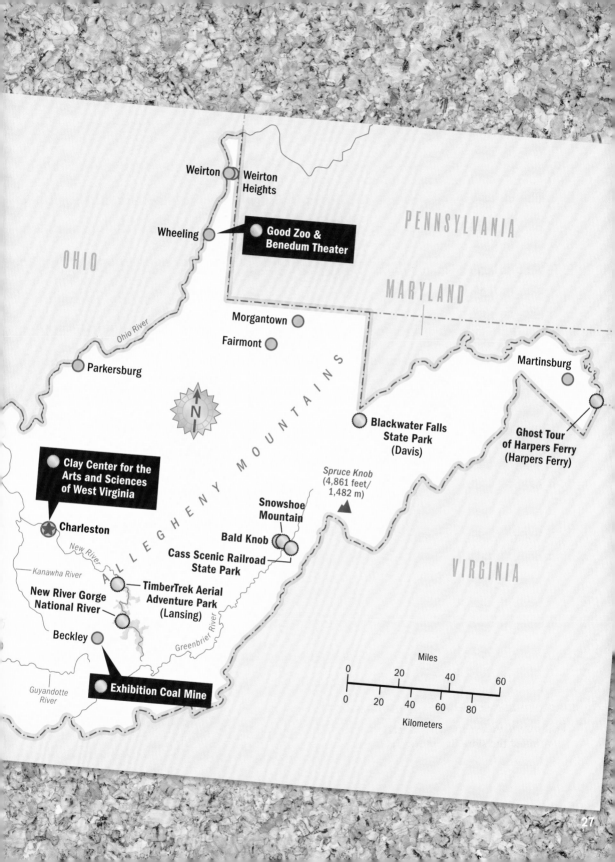

Weirton

Weirton Heights

Wheeling

Good Zoo & Benedum Theater

PENNSYLVANIA

OHIO

MARYLAND

Morgantown

Fairmont

Parkersburg

Ohio River

N

Martinsburg

Blackwater Falls State Park (Davis)

Ghost Tour of Harpers Ferry (Harpers Ferry)

Clay Center for the Arts and Sciences of West Virginia

Spruce Knob (4,861 feet/ 1,482 m)

Snowshoe Mountain

Charleston

Bald Knob

New River

Cass Scenic Railroad State Park

Kanawha River

VIRGINIA

New River Gorge National River

TimberTrek Aerial Adventure Park (Lansing)

Beckley

Greenbrier River

Exhibition Coal Mine

Guyandotte River

A L L E G H E N Y   M O U N T A I N S

Miles

0   20   40   60

0   20   40   60   80

Kilometers

WEST VIRGINIA FACTS

NICKNAME: The Mountain State

SONGS: "West Virginia Hills" by Ellen King and H. E. Engle; "West Virginia, My Home Sweet Home" by Julian G. Hearne Jr.; "This Is My West Virginia" by Iris Bell; and "Take Me Home, Country Roads" by John Denver, Taffy Nivert, and Bill Danoff

MOTTO: *Montani Semper Liberi*, or "Mountaineers Are Always Free"

FLOWER: great rhododendron

TREE: sugar maple

BIRD: cardinal

ANIMAL: black bear

FOOD: Golden Delicious apple

DATE AND RANK OF STATEHOOD: June 20, 1863; the 35th state

CAPITAL: Charleston

AREA: 24,230 square miles (62,755 sq. km)

AVERAGE JANUARY TEMPERATURE: 32°F (0°C)

AVERAGE JULY TEMPERATURE: 72°F (22°C)

POPULATION AND RANK: 1,854,304; 38th (2013)

MAJOR CITIES AND POPULATIONS: Charleston (50,821), Huntington (49,177), Parkersburg (31,186), Morgantown (30,666), Wheeling (28,009)

NUMBER OF US CONGRESS MEMBERS: 3 representatives, 2 senators

NUMBER OF ELECTORAL VOTES: 5

NATURAL RESOURCES: trees, coal, natural gas, oil, salt

AGRICULTURAL PRODUCTS: cattle, eggs, hay, apples, peaches

MANUFACTURED GOODS: chemicals, metals, lumber

STATE HOLIDAYS AND CELEBRATIONS: West Virginia Day

GLOSSARY

abolitionist: a person who wanted to put an end to slavery before the Civil War

aerial: happening in the air

exhibition: a place or an event at which objects are on public display

gorge: a narrow, steep-walled canyon or passage

mantrip: a shuttle that usually runs on tracks like a train, used to take coal miners in and out of a mine

natural resource: material produced by the Earth

planetarium: a building or a room that projects images of stars, planets, and moons onto a dome-shaped ceiling

sawmill: a factory where logs are cut into boards

LERNER

SOURCE

Expand learning beyond the printed book. Download free, complementary educational resources for this book from our website, www.lerneresource.com.

FURTHER INFORMATION

Doeden, Matt. *Finding Out about Coal, Oil, and Natural Gas*. Minneapolis: Lerner Publications, 2015. Learn how people collect some of West Virginia's energy resources, including coal, oil, and natural gas, and the effects of these resources on our environment.

Fedyszyn, Kirra. *The Hatfields and the McCoys*. New York: PowerKids, 2015. Read more about the legendary Hatfield and McCoy family feud.

Owings, Lisa. *West Virginia*. Minneapolis: Bellwether Media, 2014. Explore the geography and culture of West Virginia.

West Virginia Legislature
http://www.legis.state.wv.us/educational/Kids_Page/fun_facts.cfm
Read fun facts about West Virginia and its state capitol.

West Virginia State Parks & Forests
http://www.wvstateparks.com/
Browse through all of the information you'll need for your visits to West Virginia's many state parks and forests.

WV Travel4Kids
http://www.wvcommerce.org/travel/wvtravel4kids/default.aspx
Check out this site for even more ideas on fun things to do in West Virginia.

INDEX

PHOTO ACKNOWLEDGMENTS

The images in this book are used with the permission of: © Jon Bilous/Shutterstock Images, pp. 1, 5 (top), 7 (top); NASA, pp. 2–3; © Laura Westlund/Independent Picture Service, pp. 5 (bottom), 27; © Les Palenik/Shutterstock Images, p. 4; © David Jones CC 2.0, pp. 6–7; © Fuse/Thinkstock, p. 7 (bottom); Shayfan, pp. 8–9; © Vicki Smith/AP Images, p. 9 (top); John Collier/Farm Security Administration/Office of War/Library of Congress, p. 9 (bottom) (LC-USF34-084069-E); © Eric DiNovo/The Daily Telegraph/AP Images, pp. 10–11; © Jeff Gentner/AP Images, p. 11 (top); © Everett Collection/Newscom, p. 11 (bottom); Gary Hartley/National Park Service, pp. 12–13; National Park Service, pp. 13 (bottom), 13 (top); © Don Smetzer/Alamy, pp. 14–15; © Bobistraveling CC 2.0, p. 15; © Adam J./Shutterstock Images, p. 14; © Andre Jenny/Stock Connection Worldwide/Newscom, pp. 16–17; © Kenny Kemp/Charleston Gazette/AP Images, p. 16 (top); © Robert Wojcieszak/The Daily Mail/ AP Images, p. 16 (bottom); © Adventures on the Gorge, pp. 18–19, 18, 19; © Oglebay Resort, pp. 20–21, 21 (top), 21 (bottom); © William S. Kuta/Alamy, pp. 22–23; © amateur photography by michael CC 2.0, p. 22; Small, Maynard, & Company/Library of Congress, p. 23 (LC-USZ62-106337); © Gary C. Tognoni/Shutterstock Images, pp. 24–25, 24; © Vladislav Gajic/Shutterstock Images, p. 25; © Globe Turner/Shutterstock Images, p. 26; © Mariusz S. Jurgielewicz/Shutterstock Images, p. 29 (top); © Doug Lemke/Shutterstock Images, p, 29 (middle left); © Zigzag Mountain Art/Shutterstock Images, p. 29 (middle right); © Abemos/Shutterstock Images, p. 29 (bottom).

Front cover: © Joe Tabb/Dreamstime.com (Cass Scenic Railroad State Park); AP Photo/The Daily Telegraph, Eric DiNovo (ATV on the Hatfield-McCoy Trail); © appalachianview/Deposit Photos (Blackwater Canyon); © kansasphoto/flickr.com, CC BY 2.0 (Harpers Ferry); © Laura Westlund/Independent Picture Service (map); © iStockphoto.com/fpm (seal); © iStockphoto.com/vicm (pushpins); © iStockphoto.com/benz190 (corkboard).